TRUST ME I'M AN ESTATE AGENT

The Estate Agent's Manual

Scribbled by Damien Sinclair Jefferies

Published by High Street Publishers
2015

Published by High Street Publishers
6 Shrewsbury Terrace, Butts Hill, Sheffield, S17 4AN

@agenttrustme

ISBN 978-0-9932092-0-8
also available as an ebook

Cover design by JD&J Book Cover Design

Interior design and layout by Daisy Editorial

– PROVISO –

This guide is based on English law and practice, and in some instances the particular quirks of property ownership and estate agency in London. If you are based elsewhere, remember that practices, procedures and laws may be different!

– CONTENTS –

QUICK BACKGROUND

At the ripe old age of 41 (might be 43 by the time this is published!) I decided during a midlife crisis (which might now be over) to write a book, in between getting tattooed, riding motorbikes and planning a trip down Route 66. With a change of career long overdue, a shift from born salesman to an author with an undoubted long and successful book-writing career in front of me seemed perfect.

The initial problem was deciding on what bestseller I should write. A romantic novel? A sex book along the lines of '68 shades of grey and I owe you one'? A murder mystery? (Although there was nothing mysterious about why I could have murdered a few negotiators and applicants over the years…) And then it hit me. I would write a book about the only subject I know a little something about: The Estate Agent.

Estate agent: *agent concerned with the valuation, management, lease and sale of property; the administrator of a large landed property acting on behalf of its owner; estate manager.*

Having worked with some very colourful and interesting characters in the property industry for over twenty years, sharing my experiences and teachings between the covers of a book seemed like the right thing to write about.

They say that prostitution is the oldest profession in the world, dating back as far as 18 BC (Before Cluttons, 1837). But, whatever way you choose to look at it, selling was involved at some point in the transaction, so I would argue that the art of selling is at least two minutes older! Also, someone must have acquired the property in which the negotiated deed took place by way of purchase or lease…

With so many centuries under its belt, how hard could it be to find endless content on the art of selling? There's certainly more content than in Katie Price's 43rd biography. (Or is that her 43rd marriage? I get 'confused.com'.)

There has always been a need for estate agents since documented land ownership began, starting with the Domesday Book in 1086, necessitated by the after-effects of battle and survival to today's anticipation of those all-important 'who's the daddy?' DNA tests and lie detector results kindly provided by Jeremy Kyle. Well, well, well, even Charles Darwin would be proud.

Having not set pen to paper much or read many books by intellectual writers, as you will no doubt discover as you read on, I have had to draw deep on my personal experiences. One of my inspirations was a delightful teenage new car salesman with a slightly humorous swagger, which was obviously unintentional. "What would it take for us to do a deal today?" came the sales pitch, you know the one from the 'How could I say no?' presentation, better known in the industry as 'the close'. (And no, it doesn't mean close the door and don't let the fuckers out until they buy something!) I'm now learning how to type on a word processor – sorry, I mean laptop – having delusions of completing this newly inspired work: Training Manual of the Year… the Nobel prize… and the winner is…!

To say I was a natural born salesman may be doing myself an injustice. In my first school report that actually meant something – not "Damien splashed red paint on a canvas today entitled Monster in my Closet", also better known as the paper fridge magnet that no doubt today would induce a visit from social services – when my parents started to scrutinise its complete contents, down to my PE attendance, they found a comment under the heading 'Overall Comments': "Damien is the type of person you would expect to turn up at a rugby match wearing a camel coat and smoking a cigar." Only fitting that Del Boy, one of our greatest all-time salesmen, would later name his son after me; I was no older than 11 years old.

I soon learnt that everything in life involved selling in some way. My late father was a manufacturer by trade but without sales he had no business. I will never forget his favourite quote: "When the one great scorer comes to put a mark against your name he will not ask whether you won or lost but how you played the game." I believe it's attributed to an American sportswriter in the early part of the twentieth century, but my father used it to his advantage regularly, so often in fact that we contemplated having it on his gravestone. It's a similar argument to some of the shenanigans regularly practised by estate agents just simply not being cricket!

My father was very superstitious. We were never allowed to place keys on a table. Thanks for that Dad, perfect for my career choice. Even with such hurdles to overcome I persevered.

I won't bore you with the years in between paint splashing canvases and when I left what I thought at the time was a prison that happened to have the words 'Public School' highlighted on a board outside, nor do I want to write an autobiography, so let's skip to the crunch. With such a privileged education, I did what was expected of me: I became an estate agent (unless my publisher tells me otherwise)!

This is where it all started, my deep affection for sales. I will always remember my first day as a property professional, or what we used to call, back in the day, The Apprentice. However much it conjures up glamorous images of suit-wearing boardrooms and a job for life boasting a £100,000-a-year salary, as long as you avoid the finger-pointing *capo di tutti capi* (a mafia term – the boss of bosses) uttering the words "you're fired", it was certainly nothing like as glamorous as that. Instead, I learnt how to give Mr Chan a 'Leslie Crowther' (see Chapter 14).

Necessity to invention, invention to innovation, innovation to production and production to consumption. I was never going to invent anything, although I did have some experience once when my father decided he would patent the toothbrush-and-toothpaste-in-one. I'm not sure if that's toothpaste with a brush or a brush with toothpaste, but I think after some serious deliberation and extensive patent investigations he decided against it.

I was sure innovation was not the answer, and I was never going to get my hands dirty, so, having been born with the gift of the gab and two feet that walked at ten to two (for those of you who don't understand ten to two it means ten minutes before you are back at your desk, phone in hand, ready to ring the next applicant), that left one place for me: somewhere in between production and consumption.

My first job as The Apprentice was in an area called Hammersmith, a vibrant part of West London. I will never forget the long-drawn-out interview; it lasted all of a minute! Thank goodness I had Latin as my second language and went to all of those after-school athenaeums. My mother always said it would come in useful one day.

The interview went along the lines of: "Can you drive?" and "Have you got a car?"

I believe my answer was "*Raedam gubernare possum*", and I was hired.

The manager of the office was no taller than five feet and had the same time-telling two feet that were obligatory back then. He wore the compulsory Hugo Boss suit, a uniform bought on the Austin Reed pay monthly account card, Church's loafers with tassels and white towelling socks. The first words spoken to me on that life-changing Monday morning were, "Sit in front of me, young blood, and listen to everything I say."

I wouldn't say I learnt a lot, or indeed much at all, sitting in the old pink leather chair in front of a man who was only five years older than me and who kept referring to me as "son", but I did learn one of the most important things about being an estate agent: passion, and possibly a sense of humour…!

My journey began around the same time that it was almost more important to sell someone a pension-linked mortgage attached to an endowment with a life policy, not only for the applicant but also the extended family, rather than sell the house. I always wondered back then why it said 'estate agent' above the door instead of financial services; maybe the clue was in the 'regulated by' (it's not the song performed by Warren G). I often wonder what happened to all those mortgage brokers with the same shining personalities as those fussy tea-drinking accountants.

Fortunately for me I worked for, wait for it… an independent! Independent because we were not owned by a financial institution, but we were certainly getting commissions to refer to one:

"I am looking to buy a house."

"That's nice, sir. Do you have your mortgage arranged, and would you like a pension?"

It was a good time to work in the industry. We had just been through the recession of the early 90s; no more young upwardly mobile professional (YUPPIE) estate agents with their £50-a-minute mobile phones that looked like house bricks (no comparison intended but fitting), and certainly before *Changing Rooms*-watching Tory housewives being inspired by the forever-pregnant Sarah Lucinda Beeny, a trowel in one hand and a wee bairn in the other.

People were buying houses at no more than two and a half times their income, and with a fixed mortgage rate of 0.9 per cent given to anyone who could sign their own name (or anyone else's for that matter) there was only one way house prices could have gone: UP! So they did, at a pace of 30 new applicants a day and 20 new instructions a week. Some months we were agreeing 50 sales 'per calendar month' (a cringeworthy lettings term constantly heard on *Homes Under the Hammer* – try to avoid).

In that environment we had to learn techniques to make the day constructive, techniques that I am writing this book to share with you, and hopefully the same techniques that will inspire you through both busy and quiet housing markets.

There doesn't have to be a busy market to create activity. Remember your desk is like your own personal office and it's up to you how busy you want that office to be. It shouldn't be the manager motivating you; you have to motivate yourself. If you can't do that, try another industry. Without those sleepless nights or remembering to call someone back at three o'clock in the morning you can't be doing the job properly!

Finally, for all my sins, I opened my own estate agency in September 2006 and grew the company to three offices in Notting Hill, Bayswater and Paddington covering all aspects of the industry, including block management. I sold the company in March 2013.

Buying a house is one of the biggest emotional and financial commitments most people will make in their lives, and that certainly creates insecurities. Selling houses and letting properties is not always about delivering good news; buyers pull out, vendors want more money on exchange, the unlikeliest of tenants have taken up the second-oldest profession in the world… just some of the scenarios you will have to deal with on a daily basis.

However, through all the good times and bad times, I can honestly say it's a wonderful industry. If after reading this book you still want to be an estate agent then no doubt you will feel the same.

Enjoy.

In the words of one of my best friends, business partner and mentor, the one and only late Harry Robinson, "Sell something!"

-1-

WHY ARE YOU DOING THIS?

*T*he key to success is not made by Chubb or Yale, and is certainly not the key that fails to work on a second viewing. It's the drive and determination to *be the best at what you do*; remember that the cream will always rise to the top. If I had to work with a team who strove to be the best or a team who claimed they were commission-driven, I know which side I would choose!

An important issue that all negotiators must overcome, joking aside, is that we are NOT cold callers. Everyone calls the office for a reason and it's our job to understand that reason and guide the caller through the process.

One of the biggest weaknesses of negotiators is the Fear of Rejection. In the majority of negotiators I have worked with over the years it's the main reason they fail. On understanding that you are not forcing anyone to call the office in the first place, these fears can be eliminated.

I believe as soon as commission is involved we automatically feel that we are sales-driven, creating a barrier between us and the applicant or vendor. We tend to feel that people believe we are being deceitful to obtain a commission. If we can understand the reason why the potential applicant or vendor called the office, and we genuinely believe we have understood those reasons and are advising them from the best of our knowledge, then we are half way to overcoming these fears.

There are several questions you can ask to quickly and simply identify the requirements of the person sitting in front of you or on the other end of the phone without sounding like the archetypal estate agent (although some agents have worked very hard for that reputation over the years). I will talk you through these in subsequent chapters.

An estate agent's job is to achieve the maximum price possible for your vendor or landlord (your client) and, more importantly, with a buyer or tenant who meets the client's requirements, and within a specific or a more flexible timeframe. There are several ways to achieve this and I will cover each technique with tried and tested methods, mixed in with passion and belief in what we are selling, to whom and why. If you follow these techniques you'll be selling or letting houses in no time.

Having interviewed hundreds of potential negotiators over the years, I can honestly say that over 90 per cent have claimed that their motivation is, wait for it... money! So when I catch them staring into space at three o'clock in the afternoon dreaming about the girl in accounts, the motivation is questioned; but a swift removal of the chair and the phone tied to the side of the head with an elastic band soon gets the money-motivated back on track.

During the course of the year there is a selling cycle. At the beginning of the year you will be greeted by the 'new year, new leaf' or 'it's our last Christmas here, time to move' applicants. The summer months tend to be quieter as most families are on holiday and kids are off school. And December… who wants to move at Christmas? I have always argued that December is the best time of year to buy a house as most sellers are more negotiable if they are still on the market at this time. It's important that you stay motivated throughout the cycle as the effort you put in today generally shows results some weeks later (and media reports on the housing market tend to follow this cycle).

The true key to success is the drive to *be the best at what you do*; money becomes a good by-product. When speaking with someone on the phone you should passionately want them to feel that you are the best person they have dealt with and that you are using the two most important things god gave you on each side of your head. Eventually you will hear a smile over the phone and a connection. "Trust me, I'm an estate agent." It's the world's greatest icebreaker.

– 2 –

YOUR FIRST DAY

Iwill never forget my first day. Armed with a black-and-white instant camera, I was sent out to take landscape and portrait photos of available property, the addresses highlighted on pages photocopied from the London A–Z. We were still awaiting the invention of the satellite navigation system; you don't realise how easy you have it these days.

Two decades later, how much the world has changed. You have accepted your £75,000 OTE (on-target earnings – read the small print) salary plus a signwritten company car, a company mobile phone and maybe a company iPad. Unfortunately, there is a lot of emotional and hard work in front of you (contrary to what people think), including many late evenings and working weekends that are highly appreciated (NOT), infringing on your social life.

Being an estate agent is more than just selling or letting a property; it's dealing with people's emotions. Moving house is considered to be one of the most stressful things you can do in a lifetime. Buying a property now is more than just buying a home; it's buying into a lifestyle.

Make it your lifetime's ambition to help make the process as simple as possible through experience and local knowledge. Experience will come in time but local knowledge is a part of the job you can start learning straight away.

It's incredible how many negotiators turn up for work on the first day without any idea where the nearest train or tube station is, let alone what day of the week it is! So, before the big start day, take some time to research the area. This sort of information can be found hiding in books as well as on the internet.

There are many reasons why people move, to be closer to a tube, for example. Call me dumb but might it not be good to know where the local tube stations are located? It might be surprising to some of you that families move to be closer to good schools; again, not a bad idea to find out where the local schools are situated and which roads are within the catchment area.

Buying a house is an exciting time, and the fact that Jimi Hendrix wrote 'Purple Haze' next door may just enhance the whole process, but probably not if you were living next door at the time! (167 Westbourne Grove, Notting Hill, W11 for all those Jimi Hendrix fans.)

Before you can start matching requirements, local knowledge is essential; not only transport but also schools, restaurants, motorway access, nearest airports and good bars for after work on Fridays (only the best agents appreciate a Saturday morning hangover).

There is a lot more to selling houses than just matching bedroom requirements and prices. If this were the case I would have employed well-oiled door-opening robots that turned up on time for work every day, putting an end to sick days. Oh, what a dream come true! No more excuses as bad as cutting your mouth on a cornflake (you know who you are), which has to be the number one of all time excuses on our Best Excuses for a Day Off list, followed closely by a negotiator from the Philippines who felt he was entitled to a day off for Chinese New Year (you definitely know who you are). Personally I have always been a strong believer in mind over mucus!

I could never understand how someone suffering from food poisoning could pinpoint the exact prawn on that fateful pizza they had the night before. Prawns appear to love making drunken people sick; it's what they live for. Prawns have a lot to answer for! If the government banned prawns we could reduce sick days by as much as 70 per cent.

Furthermore, I still await an explanation from a doctor on how a twisted ankle can affect your vocal cords…

I believe the best way to learn is to jump into the deep end, and this is exactly what you need to do with the list of applicants that your new colleagues have mustered up for you on your first day. I would doubt very much that the hottest buyers currently registered in the office are going to find their way into your lap on that first day, so be prepared for the worst and stay motivated. You could be leaving a few answerphone messages (or LMTCB as they are better known in the trade: left message to call back). The best way to improve the quality of your applicants is to be the first to answer the phone and so the first to register new ones!

The first challenge of being an estate agent is how to sell a property where everyone else has failed. Assumption really is the mother of all fuck-ups! The longer you dwell on the inevitable Fear of Rejection, the greater the chance you have of failing. However, when you have no pre-conceptions and you don't judge a property, whether that's its condition, price or location, then the better chance you have of selling it. Too often negotiators become negative about certain properties and for that reason those are the properties that they don't sell.

Always pick several properties in different price ranges to go out and view. Let's face it, all estate agents are nosey; why else would we do the job? Certainly not a six-day week and working until eight o'clock every night. It's a good idea to see what you can buy in that area for the price, rather than making assumptions, especially if you are a negotiator changing area. There can be a world of difference between one property and the next. But after reading this book you are never going to judge a property again… whatevs!

I will briefly explain the Fear of Rejection. All properties come with a compromise, some larger than others, and usually this is reflected in the value of the property.

However, some compromises may reflect in how we sell the property to someone, having an effect on our enthusiasm. To be a good negotiator you must treat every property with the same enthusiasm, whether it's a flat above a restaurant or a penthouse overlooking Hyde Park.

If you believe the property to be good value you will generate far more viewings than for a property you believe to be expensive. This is human nature, but negotiators who generate the same interest in each property because they do not let their opinions affect their ability are the ones who are best at what they do.

You are not acting in the vendor's or landlord's, your clients, best interest if you make derogatory judgements about their property. Let's face it, most negotiators would struggle to buy or rent the majority of the properties they have listed, so do not judge. It's your job to see the positive side of every property and match those positives to a potential buyer or tenant.

My job, hopefully, in scribbling this book is to change your attitude from Fear of Rejection to Overcoming Objections.

So, it's the end of the first morning: you have familiarised yourself with the area, you now know every road like a London black cab driver who's just passed The Knowledge, you have viewed the entire property register and you know every price like the back of your hand.

Now you have a Danny (La Rue – clue) and it's the afternoon. Time to get to know your applicants.

3

GETTING TO KNOW YOUR APPLICANTS

Finding common ground and establishing common interests between yourself and the applicant is your first priority. That could include knowing the same people, places you have been, supporting the same football team, or the like. There will always be something you have in common.

Adapt the way in which you speak to people. Everyone is different and, as the old saying goes, people buy people. When you and the applicant are on the same level, reading from the same page, you will be surprised at how much easier the job becomes, no longer having to describe each property over the phone but just a quick, "I have got a new property on. What day are you free to view?"

Having established your new best friend, the objective over a series of viewings and telephone conversations is to find the ideal home for your applicant by getting to a compromise and Overcoming Objections.

Believe it or not, every buyer will compromise, whether they are looking to spend £250,000 or £10m.

Remember, an applicant calls or emails the office for a reason and it's your job to identify those reasons, in order of preference. So how do you do that? Firstly, the motivation.

WHY ARE YOU MOVING?

Without this information you have no chance of helping applicants to find what they are looking for. First impressions are very important in this industry and if an applicant was left with a bad impression by the previous negotiator there is a good chance you will fall into LMTCB territory. I will cover securing a new applicant in the next chapter, so for now back to your red-hot inherited buyers. It's still only your first day, and remember what they say about Rome.

You can establish the initial motivation by looking at the reason why the applicant called the office in the first place. Basic requirements fall into some common categories:

FTB (first-time buyer)

A complex creature who generally starts with misguided enthusiasm. We all set out with visions of Buckingham Palace and the Hanging Gardens of Babylon outside our window, encouraged by the evolution of estate agent photographs that can turn a studio flat into a Soho warehouse apartment.

Honesty is the only policy. If applicants cannot afford what they are looking for, advise them accordingly and make alternative suggestions, but in a courteous manner and certainly do not be condescending.

The quickest way to establish exactly what the applicant is looking for, and whether it's achievable, is to view no more than three different properties, two within the registered price range and one slightly over.

NTS (nothing to sell)

Similar to the FTB in that they can proceed immediately, these applicants may currently own another property and the latest purchase requirement is for a bijou pied-à-terre (not a shoe label but a small residential unit located some distance from their primary residence!), a rental investment or the like, as long as they don't have to sell their current property to buy another. (However, I have heard that story a lot and nine times out of ten they can't actually afford it.)

PTSOM (property to sell on market)

Highly motivated but without the sale of their house they are not in a position to proceed. The longer their property is on the market, the greater the chance that their house could be worth less than they originally thought, therefore the property they are looking to buy will have to cost less.

With local property that is on the market you must make a note in your diary to call every week, first to check if there has been any change in circumstances from PTSOM to U/O (see below), and more importantly to secure the instruction. If the property has been on the market for a long time, chances are they may be willing to change agent, especially if you find the property they want to move to.

PTS (property to sell)

Similar to PTSOM but, without placing their property on the market, the likelihood is they will lose the 'perfect' property they find every time. The least motivated of all the applicant types, or else they have listened to bad advice, and there is plenty of that in this industry. The quicker you can establish the selling price, the quicker you can establish the buying price. This can only be discovered by placing the property on the market, and that's good advice!

U/O (under offer)

The most motivated of all the applicants. Having agreed a sale on their own property they are now in a position to proceed at a price they know they can afford. This is the applicant that you kidnap in the car and drive round to every potential property you have available until they buy something (known as 'the close' and mentioned at the beginning of this book).

With these applicant types in mind and prior to making a call, prepare yourself for exactly what you are trying to achieve. Making a call without direction, repeating yourself or making calls with no benefit to either yourself or the applicant will lead to LMTCB. Firstly, look at the applicants' details and check that the motivation is clear (for example, downsizing because the kids have left home).

It's not uncommon for the motivation to have passed its 'sell-by date'. For example, "My landlord is selling the house I am currently living in and I have two months to move out"... but six months later they are still registered. You must revisit the motivation in these cases and that's where you will start the conversation with your inherited applicants.

HOW LONG HAVE YOU BEEN LOOKING?

The second most important question. Applicants who have been looking for a long time will generally have lost their motivation. A lot can happen, both personally and financially, over a 12-month period (or a week in politics, according to Harold Wilson, but then what did he know?).

House prices generally rise by 10 per cent over a year, which is theoretically three and a half times inflation at a rate between 2.5 and 3.5 per cent. The UK housing market is very seasonal and tends to move more dramatically in either direction, but over a sustained period the 10 per cent annual increase rule generally applies.

The longer applicants are looking in a rising market, the smaller the affordable properties will become, hence the loss of motivation. If the applicants you have in front of you have seen in excess of 20 properties without being interested in any of them, I can guarantee the problem's not the properties they've been viewing, it's the other fear... the Fear of Commitment.

As we have established that buying a property is the biggest commitment people will make in a lifetime, apart from marriage perhaps, and assuming that at all stages of the buying process buyers have second thoughts (see the similarities?), you can understand why it is important to establish a relationship and discuss the 'elephant in the room'.

There is no point in showing your applicants further properties if they are not ready to take on such a commitment. Discuss the reasons why they have the Fear of Commitment and try to resolve the issues before pressing them to look at any further properties.

If your applicants believe the property market is going to crash in the near future, I very much doubt they are going to buy a property any time soon. Unless you ask the next simple question.

WHAT DO YOU THINK OF THE CURRENT HOUSING MARKET?

You could be wasting your time and that of your applicants until you overcome this major objection.

Overcoming Objections is about more than the number of bedrooms, the area or the distance from a tube station. Without knowing the personal circumstances of your applicants, how can you advise them correctly?

If your applicants are currently renting you must find out what they are paying in rent. Applicants paying expensive rents are highly motivated to move, whilst applicants paying low rents are the least motivated. For example, if an applicant is paying £200 per month in rent for a room in a nice house, what's the motivation to move and take on a mortgage?

As I will continue to impress upon you, there is always an underlying reason why the applicant called the office in the first place.

It could be the landlord selling the property, the lack of what's commonly next to godliness (plenty of that in rental accommodation!), that the applicant feels it's the right time to buy, or that his girlfriend feels it's time he should leave home!

Whatever the reason, it will help you to determine the urgency of the applicant. For those of you who like a challenge and are now determined to *be the best at what you do*, try selling to an over-50 FTB still living with parents. Good luck!

Us Brits have an issue when talking about our finances and tend to be very guarded. However, because of the current mortgage lending climate it's imperative that the buyer has a mortgage approved in principle up front. Gone are the days when you could get a mortgage offer in a week. The restrictions on lending have increased with the credit crunch caused by the self-cert mortgage, both here and in the United States, and helped by soft property valuations by surveyors.

The majority of negotiators struggle to deal with this topic but it's more important now than it has ever been. Don't waste your time showing applicants a plethora of properties if they are unable to obtain a mortgage.

Once you have established that the applicant you managed to get on the phone has been looking for five years and has seen over 400 properties (I never let exaggeration get in the way of a good story) and is still very motivated, the best question for day one is the next one.

WHAT'S THE BEST PROPERTY YOU HAVE SEEN AND WHY?

A simple question that, if delivered correctly, should answer all the standard boring questions without having to ask them.

For example, take this response:

"The best I've seen is a two-bedroom Victorian apartment on [a specific street]. It was on the first floor with high ceilings, original features and a roof terrace, on the market for £750,000 and in need of some modernisation."

You have now established how many bedrooms they are looking for, what style of property, the ideal floor, that they want some outside space, they are prepared to do some work and the price range.

Although you may not know the property register well enough at this point to identify a direct comparison, there is no harm in asking your colleagues if there are any available properties on the books that match that description.

Surely it can't be that easy?

Another great tactic on day one is discovering whether the applicants' requirements have changed, generally because they are having to compromise, having seen several properties.

The classic mistake is the "My applicant won't look at basement flats" type of assumption. I would say that the majority of buyers who bought basement flats started out with the intention of never buying a property below ground level, but requirements can change constantly.

Basements flats tend to be larger for the money and generally have their own front door, with lower service charges as you are not contributing to maintenance for the common areas and a lift (if applicable). A good example of Overcoming Objections.

The negotiator who continues to check back on the original requirements and asks this question first will get the sale. As an exercise on day one, ask every applicant.

IF I SHOW YOU THE PERFECT PROPERTY, WHAT WOULD BE YOUR MAXIMUM PRICE?

I guarantee that at least half of your applicants will tell you a higher or lower price than they are currently registered at, which means your colleagues have been showing them the wrong properties.

"The more outgoing calls you make, the more incoming calls you will receive."

So said Albert Einstein (only kidding!).

PS

- Wear something different that helps people to remember you by.
- If an applicant calls the office and doesn't remember your name, read this book again!

4

REGISTERING NEW APPLICANTS

First impressions are of the utmost importance. Houses do not sell themselves and vendors do not instruct just any agent on the toss of a coin. Brand awareness is not just about advertising in magazines and driving signwritten Mini Coopers. It's the complete package, including the service provided by each member of staff, and (my favourite) that crucial word of mouth.

Reputation and brand awareness have a lot to do with you as an individual. Personal recommendations will help you to sell a property and get instructions, but guess what? That's just the start. The manager's job is not just to obtain instructions (get a new property to sell). The service you provide plays a significant role in the whole process. If applicants have a property to sell, why would they instruct anyone else but you? You need to be driven to *be the best at what you do.*

When people walk through the door of your office you must STAND UP and greet them.

You must always be the first to answer the phone and the first person to STAND UP.

You will no doubt be positioned at the back of the office when you first start, but if you see someone walking towards the door, STAND UP and greet them.

Why? Try walking into an office where no one stands up and staff just smile at you from their desks. In the words of *Only Fools and Horses*, you feel like a right plonker, Rodney!

Some agents dive in by asking for details such as name, home address, work address, home telephone number, mobile number, office number, office email address, home email address, eye colour, inside leg measurement… How boring can it get? Let's face it, that's about as useful as a speed hump in a cemetery.

Personality is the one thing I can't teach you, but I can make you sound a lot more interesting to talk to. (As the saying goes, I can't polish a turd, but I can certainly roll it in glitter!)

No wonder more and more applicants register online now. Imagine speaking to five different estate agents asking you the same questions over and over again. We are trying to sell houses; we're not a bloody call centre…

Having beaten everyone else in the office to the phone, your first question (obviously after establishing it's a new applicant) should be as follows:

WHY ARE YOU MOVING?

We are now opening with a conversation; already you have broken the mould. Now you can continue with seven more simple questions that will help you to obtain most of the information you need to help new applicants in their search:

- What's your current situation?
- How long have you been looking?
- What are you currently paying in rent (if relevant)?
- What's the best property you've seen and why?
- If I show you the perfect property, what's the maximum price you would pay?
- What are your views on the current housing market?
- What's your financial position? Do you have a mortgage arranged?

Once you have those answers, consider the next question:

WHAT SHOULD THEY VIEW NOW?

This is not a question for your applicants but a very good exercise for you after procuring answers to the above. Look at the property listings you have available and write the addresses down, with an explanation as to why you chose those specific properties. This will help you to start listening to your applicants and to follow a train of thought whilst in conversation regarding their requirements. Try to envision where you see the applicants living and ask questions relevant to the properties you have in mind for them.

Arrange a time to view three properties, or more than three if they are U/O. You should always arrange a viewing tour with any new applicants. Do not settle for an "Email me the details first and I will get back to you" response. Suggest looking at three properties, all slightly different, to establish the type of property they can realistically afford within their price range.

Once you have arranged the viewing it's time to take their personal details. You must register as many contact options as possible. Daytime, home and mobile numbers are all important, plus personal and business email addresses.

Social media and up-to-date systems are essential tools for the job today, but without entering the correct information they are rendered useless.

Time management is also essential. Why waste time sending out emails when the technology can do this automatically? There is nothing worse than a quiet office echoing to the sound of typing fingers. Not on my watch – pick up the phones!

I will cover daily structure and time management more fully in the next chapter. In the meantime, make sure you have all the contact details for your applicants. There is nothing worse than being instructed on a new property that you know is ideal for an U/O applicant who is on holiday for two weeks, but it's multi-agency (with more than one agent instructed to sell it) and you only have a work number. If you were my negotiator and this happened you would certainly be off for more than two weeks – try a lifetime.

Having mastered the art of registering an applicant, which will come with experience, you will be able to take that information, digest it (known as Fat Fridays in our offices, especially Bayswater) and come up with the perfect property. I once worked with a negotiator who had been in the industry for 20 years, and she could almost tell what someone was going to buy as they walked through the office door. I don't know about an estate agent; she was more like a clairvoyant! Sorry, I can't teach you that method – buy a book by Mystic Meg!

Learn to eliminate certain properties from an applicant's search. A simple example would be an apartment located on the third floor without a lift being unsuitable for a pregnant woman, not because of the stairs whilst she's pregnant but because it's not ideal for buggy storage, baby accessories or carrying a baby in one hand and shopping in the other up three flights of stairs every day. A ground or first floor apartment would make a lot more sense. Perhaps a compromise for a smaller apartment in return for quality of life.

Another example of matching applicants' requirements would be a family of four with two dogs looking for a family home. My first thought would be not on a main road. Simply, if you return home with a car full of shopping bags, screaming kids and muddy dogs with no spaces to park the car outside the front of your house, who or what would you take into the house first? The shopping, the kids or the dogs? The answer is none of the above as it's the wrong house for them. If the house had a small drive with a gate they could close then the answer would be simple – it wouldn't matter which went first.

Discuss this kind of thought train with your applicants and they will appreciate your understanding of their requirements.

Moving home is undertaken in most cases to improve quality of life and it's an agent's job to identify what that means for each applicant. There is nothing more frustrating to applicants than an estate agent who always suggests properties that don't match their specific requirements. Back to the old LMTCB! You have been learning to put a square brick in a square hole since you were knee high to a grasshopper, so don't change now.

Whilst I appreciate emailing is an integral part of the job today it can and will break down the art of communication. However nicely you can prepare a set of property details with the use of a wide-angled camera lens and walk-through tours, no one will usually buy from a set of details alone. (I can think of a time when that has happened, but don't bank on it happening to you as it's more likely you'll see Halley's comet twice.)

Closing a sale is not about telling the applicant that the property is cheap or the vendor is desperate to sell, but a combination of viewings and conversations that lead to the ideal property. If a previous property you viewed has sold then tell the applicants, and justify the reason for the valuation of the next property.

Everyone compromises. By narrowing the search and helping applicants set their sights on realistic prospects (not telescopic ones, although there have been a few applicants and negotiators I wouldn't mind seeing them through), by eliminating the least important requirements and reiterating the right reasons why the buyers should move, that's what we call 'the close'! This process is not possible should you choose the easy option and continue to communicate with your applicants via email.

Having worked in offices where the majority of the staff choose to email, I can tell you the atmosphere is deadly. It's hard to be enthusiastic when making phone calls from a morgue. I hate to cover old ground but someone peeking over the top of a computer saying "Hi, can I help?" should, in my opinion, be working for the council.

You should only use email for sending a set of details after having arranged the viewing appointment. As previously mentioned, if you are using your systems properly, the applicants should have already received these as part of the process. If an applicant is adamant that you email them the details first then I would always send a link to the website. Not only is it a lot quicker but it's similar to sending the entire register.

Finally, check the office email as soon as you arrive in the office and register new applicants as part of your morning routine. The majority of applicants who register by email tend not to be the most motivated, but they may just be avoiding the dreaded estate agent patter.

If it's a viewing request, you must contact the applicant first and book in the appointment before another agent makes the call.

When registering applicants who have emailed, call them and treat the conversation the same as if they had just called the office. If you need a reminder, go back to the beginning of this chapter.

5

THE DAILY STRUCTURE

*T*he first company I worked for taught me the importance of structuring your day to achieve the best results. Simply put: the more viewings, the more offers, the more sales. It would be wonderful to think that we can all naturally match people to property, but that comes with years of experience, and even then you would be surprised at what some people buy.

I once had a woman who called the office looking for a million-pound house in Chiswick. It was only when she turned up dressed in Buddhist monk's robes that we established she was on a spiritual journey to purchase a house on behalf of the Dalai Lama (not a question I usually asked when taking an applicant, but my fault nevertheless).

On that note, as the majority of people typically spend a similar part of the working day at their desks, it's 'common sense' that you MUST set aside these times in your up-and-coming busy schedule to perform what is best known as the 'ring-round' (prime time). I've certainly seen some award-winning performances over the years, some even worthy of an Oscar! It's important to structure your day into a routine, including ring-rounds, follow-ups, viewings, feedback, etc. – all terminology and jargon you will learn as you read on.

Ring-rounds (prime time) are an essential part of the job for creating viewings and getting to know your applicants. The majority of managers will not structure your day for you, so to get the best results you have to be self-disciplined and stick to the routine. Without someone looking over your shoulder it's challenging, especially if the other negotiators in the office aren't following the same structure.

Essentially, your job is to sell the viewing and sell yourself (to the devil?) whilst matching the applicant to the ideal property for the right price. Simples!

Always arrange some viewings of properties priced slightly higher than the figure at which the applicants are registered. Most applicants will complain about this process, but generally it's the property they will buy. For example, with a property on the market at £499,950 the buyer is often registered at £450,000.

Before calling your applicants regarding a new instruction, it's good practice to visit the property first to identify the positives and to see what applicant you could envision living there. (But do not visit the properties during prime time!)

You should be able to match five applicants (as a minimum) to each property off the top of your head.

Always consider the location of the property when arranging a time to view. It's not a good idea to show a property next to a school at 9am, for example, or during break time. Think about first impressions!

It's too easy to let time run away with you. If you receive a call during the ring-round not relating to this time, my advice is to call back at midday or at 4pm. If you are responsible for your own sales progression then it's even more important that you only deal with issues – and there will be issues – outside of the ring-round time.

You must call ALL applicants within the price range, even if the new instruction has two bedrooms and the applicant is looking for three. As mentioned, circumstances change, so if this specific property is not the right one, use the conversation to check the requirements you have are still correct and suggest other properties, giving reasons why.

Also use this time to update the buyer on what properties have sold recently, justifying current prices. Discuss the current market conditions and how many properties are selling.

This, ladies and gentlemen, is how you start the process of 'the close'.

Remember when asking questions to shut your mouth occasionally and listen to the answers!

Your objective is to arrange a minimum of eight viewings a day, a total of 40 viewings a week, and yes that's people not properties. If you have not reached 40 then call your applicants on the Saturday.

If in a two-hour period you cannot arrange four viewings in the morning and four in the afternoon, even without the help of new instructions and price reductions, then don't bother to read on. At the end of each week, when you add your total of viewings, be honest with yourself: anything less than 40 genuine viewings a week and you will not succeed. Most agents will not monitor this information so you must stay motivated to *be the best at what you do*.

If on some day you are struggling to find your enthusiasm (which happens to be 90 per cent of the job, by the way; the other 10 per cent is what you are learning by reading this poetry) then make the remaining calls standing up, a simple way to become more positive. If applicants remain despondent then revisit the motivation that made them contact the office. I am pretty sure they are not trying to hide their reasons from you!

Daily structure
When travelling to work in the morning take ten minutes to think about what you want to achieve that day, not what you are having for lunch or what you'll do on 'Fat Friday' as we used to call it in our offices.

Monday to 'Fat Friday'

8.30am
Morning meeting with manager. It's poor management not to have a meeting every morning to plan the day's ring-

rounds and to set the daily targets for each individual. It's the only time to share any feedback on your own property register, potential instructions and required price reductions.

9am

Call all the applicants from the previous day's viewings. On a Monday morning chase up the viewings from the weekend (follow-ups). Check and respond to emails and register any emailed applicants. You must pass on all feedback to the vendors EVERY morning without fail.

10am

Following your motivating and inspiring morning meeting with the manager you will have planned the day ahead with new instructions and possible price reductions. Remember to call EVERY applicant within the relevant price ranges. You must not leave the office at this time unless the property the applicant wants to view is multi-agency. Oh, and by the way, phones don't dial themselves, just in case you wondered.

12pm

In the words of Gordon Gekko, lunch is for wimps (*Wall Street* 1987, showing my age again) but after an exhausting, passionate and emotional two-hour ring-round you deserve a lunch break, tied in, of course, with all the viewings you have arranged over the next two hours. Return any calls relating to sales chasing (updating vendors and buyers after speaking with solicitors, covered in a later chapter).

2pm
Start the afternoon ring-round. Again, bums on seats, ladies and gentlemen. It's time to improve on those viewing figures from the morning ring-round.

4pm
Having reached your viewing target for the day you can now arrange keys, details and confirm appointments for your viewings commencing shortly. Remember the principle PPPPP (planning prevents piss-poor performance). Further sales chasing, updating the vendors and buyers.

5pm
Viewings! If you have not managed to arrange any viewings for this time then update the system with vendor and applicant feedback, send any emails and continue with sales progression updates to vendors and buyers.

7pm
CLOSED unless you have further viewings.

Saturdays & Sundays
In general, weekends are the best times for viewing properties, unless your colleagues were sharper and sold the property during the week.

However, you should not arrange viewings for a Saturday or Sunday on the preceding Monday: "Come and look at this amazing property, but don't worry, take your time coming to see it, it won't be gone…" Believe me, it happens every day.

Weekends are the best days to ring the applicants you were unable to contact during the week. Only the negotiators driven to be their best participate in this ritual.

– 6 –

THE VIEWING

My first viewing was for the lettings department (back before sharing meant more than what we do on social media and recycling was riding your bike round the block twice). It was a lovely young couple over from Australia with just their sleeping bags looking for a studio flat (go figure). I borrowed the manager's Volkswagen Clipper (the ultimate Golf convertible). I dropped the roof and off I went with a bunch of keys, a couple of addresses and a map photocopied from the London A– Z guidebook ('Strange Town' for all you Jam fans) with an orange marker pen outlining my routes (there were obviously copyright issues, but that's another story).

Six hours later I returned to the office, slightly tanned, with my two new best friends from the other side of the world armed with a holding deposit. This surely must be the best job in the world? Unfortunately, the flat had been let twice over during my tour of London and my stories of mother England. A few months later the same viewing tour would take me less than 30 minutes. Do not infringe on that all-important ring-round time (prime time), as I quickly learnt.

A wise man once taught me this about trying to pick a tie to go with a new suit: "Show me three ties and it's easy to choose; show me a stack of ties and I will be confused." On that analogy, show only three properties per viewing tour, then, based on the discussions you have during those viewings, make an appointment for a further three viewings, and so on.

Check the viewing arrangements for each property, whether it's by appointment or keys. It may be that the keys are held with another agent or your management department, so locate the keys and have them ready in plenty of time before the viewing, as you may have to run around to get them.

Confirm the viewing time with the vendors, or with the tenants if the property is rented. There is nothing more embarrassing than walking in on an uncomfortable situation, not only for you but also for the applicants, and it could cost you the instruction.

I once walked in on a couple fornicating on the living room floor (better known in Queen's Park as a 'nooner'). I will never forget a top floor flat on Blythe Road in West Kensington. I backed up slowly and walked down the stairs (all four floors) as for some reason I thought it would be a good idea to press the buzzer, just in case. (I once had an applicant called Justin Case!) Why? Maybe it's the devil in me. The vendor answered and told us to come up (really). You will not be surprised to know that the applicants didn't buy the flat from the rosy-cheeked, mid-afternoon dressing-gown-wearing vendors, but it was because the bedroom was too small!

The majority of the selling process is carried out on the phone prior to the viewing. This is crucial time spent listening to the applicants and keeping them motivated that you have finally found the ideal property.

You should always arrive ten minutes before the applicants. Go through the following checklist, remembering that first impressions count. Some people can tell whether they are going to buy a property seconds after walking through the front door, so presentation is of the utmost importance.

- Open curtains.
- Turn on lights if necessary.
- Open windows for five minutes.
- Pick up the post off the floor both in the property and in the common areas.
- Tidy around, pick up towels off the bathroom floor.
- Have the front door open as it's welcoming; struggling to open the door when standing with the applicants leaves a bad first impression, and if you have just discovered you have brought the wrong keys... LMTCB.
- If the neighbours are arguing turn up the stereo (only kidding, whistle!).

When showing applicants around it's your job to point out the features and benefits that the house or flat has to offer. For example, original features, storage areas, cupboards, a naked couple on the middle of the living room floor…

The majority of your applicants will know what a bathroom and a kitchen look like so I suggest you don't point these out!

Explain why you chose this property for them based on the requirements they gave you. The two things you can't change about a property are its location and what floor it's on, but you can change the layout and the decor, build an extension, design a new kitchen or bathroom, or build an infinity pool (although swimming for hours and not getting anywhere I find pointless).

Talk through what improvements you think could be made to the property that would benefit the applicants. Simple paint colours can transform a property significantly, even adding value. (But possibly not hanging doors the other way round, Shane, but again that's another story…)

We as a nation are becoming more European in our tastes. Some of you may not remember but we have gone from carpets on our bathroom floors to spending more time living and socialising in our kitchens.

Young families generally benefit from an open-plan kitchen with a play area for the kids, so perhaps suggest adding a conservatory (subject to planning consents). This is what I mean by making suggestions to help the applicants envision living in the property.

Ask the question, "Could you see yourself living here?"

Talking of kids, when carrying out viewings always keep an eye on those passion-killing rug rats. I once showed a beautiful house in Chiswick, forgetting that there was a child, who was off with a handful of crayons decorating the walls like Banksy; an expensive viewing!

It's also been known for them to appear with all kinds of battery-operated objects they find underneath the bed, generally when the vendors are discussing how much they have enjoyed living there. Really, you have been warned!

I would advise that you should always meet the applicants in the office the first time you arrange a viewing tour. It's not only good practice to first show them the details of the properties you are about to view and discuss why you think it's worth seeing the ones you have chosen, but also importantly it's good for security.

I always preferred to meet applicants in the office on our first viewing tour and then drive with them from property to property. It's a good time to elaborate on their requirements, and if from talking you have an epiphany and there is another property that you feel may be ideal then return to the office at the end of the tour and collect the keys and add it to the tour. But remember, any more than three viewings per tour becomes confusing.

If you have lined up a property that the applicants do not want to see you must inform the vendors or tenants immediately. Most vendors will take time to prepare their home and tidy up. How would you feel if an estate agent arranged a time with you and then didn't turn up and didn't call? Another easy way to lose an instruction.

For the vendors, selling a house is just as emotional as buying one. Bear in mind, though, that the more properties the applicants see overall, the easier it will be for them to make a decision when they see the right one, so encourage them to view enough to compare.

Saturday viewings are the most popular but remember not to arrange a weekend viewing at the beginning of the week unless it's a first-time viewing tour. You must create an urgency when arranging an appointment to view a house; by arranging an appointment for five days later (especially in the London market) you are giving the impression that the house or flat is not that saleable.

Back in the day, Saturday viewings were carried out with military precision. We would arrange no less than 50 viewings between 10am and 4pm with an army of 'Saturday viewers' (people employed just to carry out viewings on a Saturday).

Friday afternoons were spent arranging appointments and keys with vendors and tenants so the next day would run smoothly. (OK, military precision might be a slight exaggeration.)

One of the negotiators in the office used to work as a croupier in a London casino, so he would entertain the applicants with card tricks as they waited for the next red-faced huffing-and-puffing Saturday viewer to return. It was chaos.

I remember taking an applicant to a four-bedroom semi-detached house instead of a two-bedroom flat in need of work; the only thing they had in common was that they were on the same street. The price difference was a shade under one million pounds. So obviously on Monday morning the applicants were waiting outside the office with a cheque book ready to make an offer at the asking price… I finally got hold of them on the Wednesday afternoon to apologise for the mix-up only to be told that the fourth bedroom was too small anyway and the garden faced the wrong way! (There is no pleasing some people. I believe ten years on they are still looking – pass me my telescopic sight…)

I firmly believe that negotiators in an office should be slightly competitive but most certainly should work together to make the office more efficient. 'Block viewings' is the terminology we use for several viewings arranged at the same property at the same time, or at slightly staggered times. Especially with new instructions, it's helpful to arrange block viewings and take it in turns to carry them out.

Three negotiators carrying out block viewings on three separate properties in one evening is far more efficient than the individual negotiators trying to meet, swap keys and make each appointment on time. However, the majority of prospective buyers prefer not to view properties at the same time as other buyers, so staggered times are preferable, otherwise it could lead to a… you've guessed it, LMTCB.

THE ART OF NEGOTIATING

Being a negotiator is, in my opinion, the best part of being an estate agent. People will always buy people – your shining personality, chatting over the phone or the conversation with an applicant sitting in front of you will always be worth more than a thousand emails.

The key to being a good estate agent is knowledge. Knowledge will instil confidence. One thing to always remember before you start negotiating is that this is the biggest purchase that most people will make in their lifetime. Respectfully return everyone's call when you say you will, make sure honesty is always your best policy, and always underpromise and overachieve.

I once had a vendor who lived abroad who called me in the office to ask whether I would put his bins out as a favour, which I did that afternoon and thought nothing more about it. You may think I'm talking garbage but I learnt one of the most important things the following day. The vendor called to check that I had indeed done what he had asked, and in a nonchalant manner I replied, "Yeah, yeah." You would have thought the world had come to an end.

The manner in which we deliver ourselves is how we will be perceived, rightly or wrongly. The fact of whether I had or hadn't placed the bins outside was now irrelevant as the vendor was taken aback by my response.

Perception is very important. It's an old cliché but do put yourself in the other person's shoes and think how you would like to be dealt with.

So here you are having taken the applicants' details and requirements perfectly, showed them the perfect property and they now want to make an offer. As it's your first time, you will probably fall over yourself, stutter and accept any offer made; it's similar to losing your virginity, isn't that right, Andre? (How was Chinese New Year?)

There are some very important considerations when taking an offer. The only price that you know is likely to be acceptable is the asking price. By suggesting any other price to the applicants you are mentally repricing the property, and this will only make your job a lot harder if you need to negotiate further.

By all means suggest making the offer anyway, but NEVER imply it could be accepted. The applicants must not leave the negotiation table believing there is a chance that their offer will be accepted. Ideally, you want them working out what their next increased offer will be.

A series of offers that have not been accepted helps to realise the true value of the property and also helps to guide the vendors to the correct maximum selling price by way of further offers or a price reduction.

Should the property have other offers, disclosing them is not illegal, contrary to what most estate agents will say, but is morally wrong. Furthermore, it mentally reprices the property again, with a "Why pay more than the next person?" attitude. Generally, people are like sheep and feel more comfortable following someone else.

On receipt of the offer you need to clarify the applicants' position. You should of course already know this, having had several discussions over the phone and a series of viewings.

It's good to know whether the buyers have arranged a mortgage sum because, in real terms, for every £10,000 offered it will cost them somewhere between an extra £20 to £50 per month, but this is perhaps a small price to pay for happiness (based on today's rates). I can't remember what the latest going rate is for happiness but this sounds a lot less than a good night out or not much more than a couple of packets of cigarettes!

Below are the main points you need to cover when taking an offer on behalf of your vendors:

- Timescale.
- Is the mortgage arranged, and if so what is the deposit (loan to value)?
- Which bank (as this has a bearing on surveyors and mortgage offer turnaround time)?

- Mortgage broker's name and contact details.
- Solicitor's or conveyancer's details.

Timescale
This can sometimes be more important than the offer amount. The vendors may accept the offer on the basis that they have already found a home to move to and it fits the timescale; not all vendors are in a rush. It may be a new job start, relocating for a new school to coincide with term times, but whatever the reason it's always good to know your applicants' position as well as that of your vendors so you can match their requirements.

Mortgage
In the current climate it's important that the applicants have an offer in principle from a lender. Recent changes in regulations mean that every application goes through a stringent affordability calculation and even a gym membership could hinder the chances of obtaining a mortgage. The deposit is also important; the larger the deposit, the less the risk for the lender and the more likely they are to agree the mortgage.

Bank
The time it takes to process the mortgage varies considerably depending on the lender. Even where the buyers offer a quick completion, some lenders will not be able to facilitate this, so contact the buyers' mortgage adviser to confirm the

details and find out what the current timescale is for that specific lender.

Banks have different surveyors on their panels (the only surveyors that they can instruct to carry out surveys). A surveyor's job is to confirm to the bank that the property is correctly priced and that it's fit for mortgage purposes. For example, properties without kitchens and bathrooms are not mortgageable. (I will cover more about surveyors in a later chapter under sales progression.)

Mortgage broker

You must have the details for the broker so that you can get updates throughout the transaction, survey dates and whether there are any delays that you may be able to help with (I will cover this in more detail in a later chapter). If, however, the buyers have not instructed a broker at this stage then recommend one that you know or that someone in the office has a good working relationship with.

Solicitor or conveyancer

In my experience it's very important that you advise the buyers to instruct the correct solicitor. This can be the difference between the sale reaching completion or not.

I would always advise that buyers instruct a solicitor or conveyancer who specialises in this field. Always recommend a solicitor that you have a working relationship with. If the buyers have already spoken to a solicitor, still suggest that they speak to your recommendation before instructing.

For instance, the London property market is very different to anywhere else in the country, with a lot of defective titles and leases that some solicitors outside of London struggle to find a reasonable solution or compromise for.

Rejections

Should the offer be rejected, remember your job is to work for the vendors to achieve the maximum price possible. The applicants of today will be the vendors of tomorrow, so they may not appreciate you working hard for the vendors now but will remember to use you when they come to sell.

People generally move to an area where they have friends and acquaintances, and there is nothing better than a personal recommendation to let you know you are doing the job right. No one is going to recommend you if you try to undersell a property, and it's not a reputation you want as an estate agent. Next thing you know you will be confronted by a microphone-wielding Matt Allwright and be starring on *Watchdog* or *Rogue Traders*.

So back to the applicants to give them the news that the offer has been rejected, armed with all the reasons why they should increase their offer. That does NOT include that the vendors want more money!

Provide the applicants with details of comparable properties that have sold recently, remind them of how many properties they have seen, and reiterate why this is the best property they have seen so far and why (because it matches their requirements). Remember how much giving up a packet of cigarettes or a night out a month can help, place value on quality of life, and then SHUT UP and LISTEN! The art of negotiation involves a series of uncomfortable silences, allowing the buyers to fill those quiet moments with responses that help you to negotiate. None of this is possible by email, so NEVER ever negotiate by email!

Advising the vendors

Advising the vendors should be simple as you and your fellow negotiators have been giving them feedback after every viewing. Confirm with the vendors how many viewings you and your colleagues have had on the property, reiterate the feedback and guide them accordingly. You should provide the vendors with evidence of comparable properties that have sold in the area recently to justify why the offer should be accepted, rejected or considered.

The process of negotiation may take several days, even weeks, and may not lead to an agreement. If at any point during the negotiations you feel that the applicants are losing enthusiasm, suggest viewing other properties. They will either refocus on the purchase at hand or change their mind; either way it's better to know now than weeks down the line. What fun would the job be if the vendors accepted the first offer every time?

Buyers and vendors may change their minds for many reasons, but remember it's an emotional process and don't be a salesman. We all have friends who give unwanted advice, especially when it comes to buying a house!

It's not how long a property has been on the market but how many applicants have seen it that realises the true value. If the first applicant who views the property offers the asking price, it would not be right to advise the vendors to accept it until the majority of the registered buyers in that price range have also viewed the property. (You work for the vendors, not the applicants, but it's ultimately the vendors' decision.) There may be a good chance that the asking price for the property is too low.

Sealed bid

In some cases you may receive several asking price offers for the same property and the vendors decide to have buyers make what's called a sealed bid. Some agents seem to think that is a process for more than one offer on any property, but unless all the offers are at the asking price there is no need for this practice. It is the fairest way to establish the right buyer should they all be in a similar position and are all prepared to move to the vendors' timescales.

This is the process by which several interested parties make a closed bid by a certain time. This can be sent by email or letter as long as it fits within the time constraints, but do not let your applicants miss the deadline.

Always tell your applicants to provide the details of their solicitor with the bid or to ask their solicitor to make the offer on their behalf.

Always advise your potential buyers to make the offer an obscure figure; for example, instead of £300,000 offer

£301,102. You will be surprised how many buyers have lost out by the smallest of margins.

Make sure your applicants' details are on the offer, including their buying position, timescales, a beautiful life story. When it comes to money in this country most people don't joke. It's not always the applicant who makes the highest offer that is in the best position, so explain to your applicants that they need to be as flexible as possible.

Good luck!

– 8 –

SALES PROGRESSION (SALES CHASING)

We naturally assume that buyers know the process of buying a property. This chapter will explain the process step by step and why it's a good idea to go through it with the buyers before the whole legal business commences.

Stamp duty

I have agreed sales in the past where the buyers were unaware of stamp duty (property tax) and that this could not be added to the mortgage.

Stamp duty is a substantial amount of money that becomes payable within 30 days after completion. The buyers' solicitor will need these funds in their account by the day of completion as non-payment will result in heavy fines.

Stamp duty thresholds change so make sure you know the up-to-date levels. When I first started in the industry, stamp duty was charged at 1 per cent for any property over

£60,000, and there were certainly a few under the threshold back then.

As of 4th December 2014 you pay a percentage rate for each portion of the purchase price, not a fixed rate on the full amount:

Purchase price	*Percentage for portion*
£0–£125,000	0%
£125,001–£250,000	2%
£250,001–£925,000	5%
£925,001–£1.5 million	10%
Over £1.5 million	12%

For example: A property sold for £300,000. Nothing to pay for the first £125,000, 2% payable between £125,001 and £250,000 and 5% payable on the last £50,000. Stamp duty owed = £5,000 (effectively 1.67% of the total amount).

The legal process

Having agreed a sale, ask the vendors and buyers for details of their solicitors or conveyancers and write to all parties outlining the terms and the purchase price. Remember to recommend legal representatives you know to both parties as this will help you enormously throughout the transaction.

You must include a copy of the property details, as these will form part of the contract, and any specific agreements about timeframes and what is being included in the sale, such as kitchen appliances, blinds, curtains, etc. (Any misinformation or misrepresentation could lead to prosecution, so check the details are correct.)

Some estate agencies have departments that deal with progression of a sale once the solicitors have been instructed. However, many don't so unfortunately you will have to learn the process and how to deal with some of the most wonderful professionals associated with our industry! (NOT)

The vendors' solicitor will prepare the contract (known as 'the papers') and will send them across to the buyers' solicitor in a system called the DX (a guaranteed mail system between solicitors).

Depending on the property this may take some time, so it's always advisable for the vendors to prepare all the papers for their solicitor prior to finding a buyer. This helps to speed up the process, which on average takes 12 weeks from an agreed sale to completion.

Upon receipt of the papers the buyers' solicitor will start the searches procedure. This process can start prior to receipt of the papers, but generally most solicitors will advise their clients to wait before incurring any costs.

Applying for searches is the process of acquiring information about the interests and regulations concerning that individual property. This information is obtained from the local council, the local water supplier and the Land Registry.

The local authority search can take up to four weeks, depending on the council, and should alert the buyers to any potentially negative issues relating to the property, ranging from local conservation areas, to enforcement notices for breach of planning or building regulations.

In certain areas outside of London it would be advisable to have a mining search to show whether the property was built above an old mine.

The buyers' solicitor will obtain up-to-date title deeds to confirm that the vendors are the legal owners and whether there are any charges registered against the property, which in most cases will be a mortgage.

However, there may be other charges relating to other loans and these must be removed before the property is sold.

Alternatively, the vendors' solicitor will give an undertaking (a promise) to pay the amounts in full and have them discharged. The property can then be sold with what's known as a clear title.

If for some reason the vendors' solicitor is unable to provide a clear title then in most cases the property is unsaleable until the charges are removed.

In cases of negative equity (where the mortgage amount is greater than the value of the house) then the vendors have to pay the shortfall to the lender along with the proceeds of the sale, either before the sale or on completion.

Once the buyers' solicitor has read the papers, he or she will raise any further questions related to the information received.

Leasehold and freehold
At this point I will explain the difference between leasehold and freehold. Hopefully I will do a better job than Golden Balls did of explaining football in the Amazon jungle!

A freehold is the ownership of the building and the land on which it sits in its entirety forever. A leasehold is the ownership of the property for a period of time, commonly ranging from as low as 10 years (sometimes lower) to 999 years.

In theory, when the lease expires the property reverts to the freeholder, so the lower the lease term the more effect it has on the property's value. If a leasehold property has more than 80 years left on the lease then the value of the property is unaffected; however, when the value drops below 80 years then the value starts to become affected (known as the 'marriage value').

During the late 70s and early 80s the majority of Victorian houses in London were converted into flats. The buildings remain the property of the freeholders and leases were created for each flat; you could say it's equivalent to buying a long rental term. Each lease within the building mirrors the others in the 'dos and don'ts', the rights of the lessee (the leaseholder) and the lease term (the length of the long rental term).

The dos and don'ts are known in the industry as the 'covenants' within the lease. It is the freeholder's job to enforce these covenants. An example is no wooden floors (a breach you will come across frequently). Amendments can be made to the leases, generally at a cost payable to the freeholder, but can be expensive.

With the lease comes a lease plan (both lease and lease plan are registered with the Land Registry). The lease plan will show the layout of the property and cannot be changed without the permission of the freeholder. Removing the wrong walls within a structure could prove dangerous without the correct planning permissions and building regulations to satisfy the freeholder or an appointed surveyor.

All flats have a ground rent (a charge payable every year to the freeholder, ranging from a peppercorn rent to £1,000 upward, with reviews during the lease term) as well as a service charge. The service charge is made up of the buildings insurance and the costs to maintain the building; this could include communal gardens, lift maintenance, communal area cleaners, etc. The total cost is divided between the flats and overseen in most cases by a management company appointed by the freeholder.

Property laws and regulations are always changing, but currently leaseholders have the right to extend a lease as long as they have owned the property for more than two years and the original lease granted was over 21 years. A chartered surveyor or similar can carry out a calculation of what it might cost to extend a lease (not something as an agent you need to work out but it's good to understand the simple process).

Put simply, the lower the lease term remaining, the more valuable it becomes to the freeholder.

As the lease term decreases, the percentage in favour of the freeholder increases, calculated on the basis of the difference between the valuation of the property with a new lease and the property with the current lease.

For example, if the difference is £200,000 and there are 30 years left on the lease, the percentage could be calculated as high as 50 per cent, so a maximum extension of 90 years on top of the current lease could cost as much as £100,000.

In addition to the £100,000 there would also be a calculation for loss of ground rent, as the new extension is charged at a peppercorn rent, in other words zero, so there is compensation for the loss of revenue.

Another major issue to consider with leasehold properties is that most properties with leases under 60 years are not mortgageable; there some exceptions, but only in the affluent areas of central London.

As a result of rogue freeholders there was a change in the law in 2002 with the Commonhold and Leasehold Reform Act, which basically states that as long as it is supported by over 50 per cent of the homeowners within the building, the leaseholders have the right to manage their own building or appoint their own managing agents.

Furthermore, subject to following the correct procedures and valuations, they are able to acquire the freehold. This is more costly than obtaining the right to manage but will eliminate ground rent charges and lease extension costs, increasing the value of the properties over time. This is called 'share of freehold'. A company is set up to acquire the freehold and all the owners have a share in the company and are therefore in control of their own block management. (David, I think you win that one!)

Seller's pack

In the papers from the vendors' solicitor will be the completed property information forms or 'seller's pack'. This includes forms showing what is being left in the property and general information such as boiler service certificates, electrical certificates, damp-proofing guarantees, etc.

As most leasehold houses were converted into flats when flared trousers were on their way out and tartan skirt-wearing anarchists were jumping up and down on our newly coloured TV screens, subsequent changes over the past 40 years mean most leases are now defective (for example, missing covenants or the ability to enforce them, to the lease plan being completely different to the current layout).

The good news is that most solicitors today will cover these imperfections by way of an indemnity insurance. It can be, however, one of the main reasons why a sale will fall through (buyer or vendor pulls out of the sale) and demonstrates the importance of having a good solicitor instructed to prevent this from happening. Communication is the key to a successful sale.

The buyers' solicitor will continue to ask questions (raise enquiries) relating to the information supplied by the vendors' solicitor until both the buyers and the mortgage lender are satisfied.

The survey

Whilst the solicitor is getting on with the easy job (to all the solicitors I have worked with over the years, I sincerely don't mean that – it's been emotional!), the buyers' mortgage broker or bank is processing the mortgage application and arranging for the surveyor.

The surveyor will arrange a time to visit the property; it's imperative that you write on the file (showing my age again) the name of the surveyor, the name of the company and the type of survey and that you inform all parties when the survey is being carried out.

There are three different types of survey:

- A valuation – to value the property with no investigative report.
- Home buyer's report – a more detailed report on condition of the property including a valuation.
- A full structural survey (this cannot be carried out on a flat unless the surveyor has access to every flat within the building) – an in-depth survey including the structure from the ground to the roof.

Obviously, the more in-depth the survey is the more problems it will show, especially on a Victorian building that has been standing for over a hundred years in the beautiful British weather.

I would always advise the buyers to have a separate valuation to the home buyer's report or structural survey. If any problems are exposed, it's better for the buyer to make the decision to proceed rather than the lender. If you instruct the valuation at the same time as the home buyer's report or structural survey, there is a possibility that the lender will see the report and make a decision to place retentions on the buyers' mortgage offer (a retention is when a mortgage lender holds back part of the money until the works identified as a defect are completed).

Completion

The aim of this chapter is to make you aware of what progressing a sale entails, but don't worry, over time your experience will grow in dealing with the endless potential problems and emotions.

Communication is very important, whether it's good news or bad news. The majority of sales that fail to complete happen because the estate agent does not communicate effectively with both vendors and buyers all the way through to completion. This is how an estate agent really earns commission.

Every week during the course of the sale you MUST call the buyers' solicitor for an update on what's outstanding. Then call the vendors' solicitor to see if you can help to obtain the outstanding information. Then call the vendors, followed by the buyers, to update them.

Finally it's time for 'exchange', on average eight weeks after the buyers' solicitor has received all the information from the vendors' solicitor, all the searches are back, the mortgage offer has been received (unless the buyers are cash buyers, but the same procedures apply) and the buyers' solicitor is satisfied and ready to proceed with an exchange of contracts.

The buyers' solicitor will require 10 per cent of the purchase price as a deposit (can be less if agreed between both parties) in cleared funds in their client account (and that can be a Friday afternoon nightmare!).

The process of exchange is simply the two solicitors speaking and confirming that both parties are happy with the contract, they agree a completion date and they are holding the deposit to order. For all intents and purposes the completion date is set in stone on exchange, though it can be moved if both parties agree at a later date, but for now let's just say that's the date the new owners will take possession of the property. Possession must be what's known as 'vacant possession'; in other words, everything must be removed from the property by that date unless otherwise specified within the contract.

Now everyone can relax. There are only a few things that the solicitor needs to do between exchange and completion: carry out a search to confirm no other charges have been registered prior to completion and arrange security for the new lender if there is a mortgage.

Well done – your first sale!

What if it goes wrong?

Although it's rare, a sale has been known to 'fail to complete'. For example, the completion money doesn't arrive or the property is involved in a chain (where one house has to be sold to buy another) and the completion money doesn't reach the house at the top of the chain in time. This could be due to slow banking systems or the solicitors at the bottom of the chain not sending the money early enough.

To avoid this, the majority of solicitors I have worked with send the money the night before, especially in cases where the chain involves more than three properties. Failing to complete should not be an option. If, however, there is a failed completion then in the majority of cases the vendor will keep the deposit acquired on exchange of contracts. Furthermore, if the property is sold for a lesser amount in the future then the vendor is entitled not only to the deposit but the shortfall in the selling amounts.

The more properties involved in the chain, the more likely there will be issues during the process, for example in valuations, agreeing completion dates, etc.

So, one last time, the key is CO-MMU-NI-CA-TION.

A third of agreed sales fall through so it's very easy to get disheartened, especially if a few sales fall through at the same time. It's a lot easier said than done but do not let your mood affect the way in which you speak to people. You can hear a smile and success down the phone – that says a lot about a negotiator.

Lastly, it's very easy to get caught up in outstanding issues during the sales progression but you MUST stick to your daily structure and not miss the ring-round times – you still have other properties to sell, and the show must go on!

– 9 –

TO LET OR NOT TO LET

The third-oldest profession in the world, "Me love you long term, short term." Letting is an agreement made between two parties for one to occupy a property owned by the other for a specific period of time. In theory, letting a property is not such a commitment as buying a property, but it can be just as emotional nevertheless.

Until September 2007, lettings had always been a service us hard core salesmen would be reluctant to answer the phones for, and we definitely found taking a lettings applicant disturbing. Estate agency was all about the sales!

How wrong could we be? The majority of estate agents who avoided lettings didn't survive much past the end of that year! My new-found favourite department, the lettings department, was officially born. Sales – who needed them?

The fees were considerably less than sales fees but, with a falling sales market and a growing lettings market, from a couple of lets per week to a queue of potential tenants half way up the street, and processing 15 lets per week, we were definitely still in business.

The options were endless: let only, let and manage, manage only, rent collection – what a wonderful business that had been right under my nose for years. We subsequently branched out into the block management business, but I will explain that more in my next book!

Back to the present. It's a misunderstanding that lettings is a good way to enter into the estate agency business. I don't believe that negotiators should carry out the roles of both sales and lettings negotiator. Both jobs are very demanding in their own right and need your undivided attention.

You will find that some estate agencies prefer an individual negotiator to complete certain files before allowing a tenant to move into a property: credit checks, references, inventory, cleaning, completed contracts, gas safety checks, etc.

There is a lot of paperwork and numerous tasks that have to be completed that will impinge upon that all-important ring-round time.

Stick to the daily structure and you will continue to let property every week; stray from the daily structure and you will find that you have good and bad letting weeks, and that will affect your pay packet!

Practicalities

Having showed a potential tenant a property, ask for a holding deposit. This is generally one week's rent and will hold the property for a time subject to the paperwork being satisfactory.

This, however, does not mean that the landlords cannot change their mind or let the property to someone else if they so wish, but it does show a commitment from the potential tenant.

The majority of the tenancy contracts that you will agree will be ASTs (assured shorthold tenancy), introduced by the Housing Act 1988 to guarantee landlords possession of their property at the end of the agreed term.

For the contract to be an AST the property must be the tenant's principal home, the tenant must be an individual and the property completely separate.

Most ASTs are for 12 months with a potential break clause after six months. However, you must agree these terms between landlord and tenant; but remember, if the tenant moves out early and the landlord has paid you 12 months' commission in advance, you will have some of your commission clawed back.

The notice period for most contracts is two months, unless stated differently in the contract and agreed by both parties.

If the tenancy expires and the contract is not renewed, the tenancy enters into what's called a 'periodic tenancy'. The terms of the contract remain the same but the tenant only has to give one month's notice instead of two.

Properties can be let in three ways – unfurnished (no furniture), fully furnished (all the furniture is included, plus cutlery, plates, etc.) and part-furnished (certain items are included as agreed between landlord and tenant).

Following drawing up the agreement, and prior to the tenant taking up occupancy, you will instruct an inventory clerk to visit the property to make an independent report on the condition, the cleanliness and, if furnished, a complete inventory of what's included.

When the tenancy ends, the inventory clerk will return to the property with the report to determine normal wear and tear, missing items or any excessive damage and assess whether there should be any deductions made from the tenant's deposit.

The rule is if the property was professionally cleaned by the landlord at the beginning of the tenancy then the tenant will pay for a professional clean at the end, either paid and arranged by the tenant or by deducting the amount from the tenant's deposit (see below).

The landlord or managing agent must return the deposit (less any fair deductions) to the tenant within ten days after the end of the tenancy. If there are any disputes then the relevant amount will be protected under the tenancy deposit scheme until the dispute is resolved. The undisputed amount must be returned to the tenant within ten days; failure to do so could result in the whole deposit being awarded to the tenant.

If you find that you are renting properties for more than £100,000 a year, they will no longer be under an AST but what is known as a common law tenancy, similar to a commercial lease, and the obligations are dependent on the terms agreed by both parties.

One of the most important things about being in business, either as a director or an individual negotiator, is maintaining your reputation. It's a lot harder to build a reputation than it is to lose one. Always think whether you would be happy for potential tenants to live in your own property before recommending to a landlord to accept them as tenants.

We all love to sell or let properties but our reputation must take precedence over this animal instinct! Whether the property is managed or is let only, consider any potential problems for both your landlord and your fellow unappreciated property manager (a thankless job at the best of times).

It's important that all members of the lettings team work in harmony and help each other to build upon the reputation that you have all worked hard to establish. Patience will run thin if there are endless problems caused by poor management and bad tenants, so WORK TOGETHER!

Services

There are three main services that estate agents can offer to a landlord:

- Let only – to find a suitable tenant/tenants and carry out all the relevant paperwork necessary to complete the let.
- Let and rent collection – the same as let only but you collect the rent on behalf of the landlord and forward it.

This attracts a slightly higher fee than let only because you are taking the responsibility that the rent is paid on time.

- Managed – the complete package. As well as let and rent collection, this service includes full maintenance of the property on behalf of the landlord.

I've known a managed service include a diverse range of issues from fixing washing machines and leaking pipes, to helping a naked famous TV actress because she had put too much liquid soap in her jacuzzi bath, or a midnight call-out because the tenant couldn't find the 'on' switch on the TV remote! (Think twice before embarking on a career in property management, especially when you are handed a mobile phone on your first day with a heavily worn, almost unreadable 24-hour service number embossed on the back!)

Legalities

Having found the ideal tenants, and with them due to move into the property in a week's time, you should have a checklist of important information that if not completed could, in some cases, lead to 'a trip down the road' (prison, for those of you who live outside of London).

Every property must comply with the latest gas safety regulations. Every year without fail the property and appliances must be inspected and repaired if required by a Gas Safe-registered engineer. The compliance certificate confirming the property has passed must be supplied to the tenant within 28 days of the annual inspection being carried out (failure to do so could lead to prosecution, possibly prison or heavy fines up to £25,000).

There is a responsibility on the landlord to ensure that the electrical installation and appliances in a property are safe. I would highly recommend that every property has a PAT (portable appliance testing) report carried out prior to the tenancy to make sure all electrical appliances are safe and in working order, though it is currently not a legal requirement to do this.

It is a legal requirement to ensure that the property has an EPC (energy performance certificate), the same as for a property on the sales market, prior to marketing and that the certificate is made available for any prospective tenant. In simple terms, it shows how efficient the property is and what can be done to increase the efficiency by way of insulating the loft, double glazing, low energy lighting, or the like.

It is a criminal offence for a furnished property to have furniture that does not meet the latest fire and safety regulations. All furniture including sofas, chairs and mattresses must have a label that confirms they comply with regulations.

In order to protect the deposit taken from the tenant at the start of the let, it must be registered with a government-backed deposit scheme. Your agency will be affiliated to a deposit scheme and every deposit must be registered. The landlords may hold the deposit – as long as they provide you with the details of the scheme in which they will hold it! "Deposit? What deposit?" I've heard that one too often.

Lettings is far more regulated than sales, but organisations such as ARLA (Association of Residential Letting Agents) provide exceptional training courses and qualifications.

If you decide to embark on a career in property management because you enjoy that "What else could possibly go wrong today?" mentality, make sure you have a thick skin, a sense of humour, a fear of holidays (because you won't get a chance to take any) and stay away from cornflakes and Chinese New Year as you can't afford to take time off. Still interested…?

– 10 –

BECOMING 'DE MANAGEMENT'

"Only three things happen naturally in organisations: friction, confusion and underperformance. Everything else requires leadership."

Peter Drucker (stolen by Damien Jefferies)

Having mastered the art of negotiation (thanks to studying the previous chapters of this invaluable guide) you have now been promoted to the post of office sales manager. Not every great negotiator makes a great manager and vice versa. One thing is for sure, management can be a lonely place if the job is done properly. My father once said to me that management is not just about turning up in the morning with a key to let the staff in and locking up when they leave at night. No truer words have ever been said!

Whatever happens from now on in the office is down to you; the buck stops here, it's on your watch. If you think management is about doing *less* work, I suggest you decline the promotion.

A good manager is the difference between the office doing well and doing badly. (Just think about some of the disastrous changes at the top in the Premier League!) Blaming the staff is not an option.

When you walk into the office in the morning, have a look around: is it tidy, do the staff look well presented, do the men have their ties on, are there dirty cups on desks, is there paper everywhere…? First impressions is the name of the game throughout the industry, ladies and gentlemen.

Look sharp, and if anyone walks into the office and no one stands up, I suggest the largest stapler in the back of the head ought to do the trick, but obviously after the applicant has left the office. (Or perhaps something less likely to induce a lawsuit!)

Good managers control the atmosphere in the office, keep everyone motivated and tune in to everyone's conversations whilst having their own. Multi-tasking. I know that's a little bit harder for us lads, apparently, but a necessity nonetheless.

My first managing director used to sit downstairs and listen to our conversations by tapping into the line. The first time I heard his dulcet tones interrupt my full flow I dropped the phone and thought I had finally lost it!

I believe strongly that the team should have a meeting every morning to run through the events from the day before and structure the day ahead. Supply the negotiators with new property instructions from the day before to ring round.

You can get the best results from a ring-round when all the negotiators are calling their applicants at the same time about the same property. Sometimes it helps to hear how other negotiators are selling the property over the phone. Not to mention the competition between the negotiators to arrange the most viewings.

Having been a successful negotiator, you know what is expected of your team to do the same. Every day you must look at the diary, check that the previous day's viewings were carried out and remove those that were cancelled from the diary so they are not totalled at the end of the week. Check that the feedback is noted for every viewing and that the vendors are being updated.

Vendors should never have to call the office to ask for feedback; they must be updated weekly at minimum. You will lose instructions if you do not maintain the promised feedback. Having worked so hard to get the instruction, there is no excuse not to.

You should always micromanage the office until you feel that everyone is 'singing from the same hymn book'. All together now: "And did those feet in ancient times…"

I have worked for companies where every member of staff was so efficient that we would not hesitate to recommend each other, and that's what you should strive to achieve in your office.

Check that every applicant's details have been taken correctly the day before, and if not, pass the applicant to another negotiator until the first learns to get it right. Trust me, on that basis it won't take long before they do.

Check that negotiators are showing applicants the right properties. Ask them to explain why they are showing those specific properties; this will help them as they develop in the job to think about what they are trying to achieve from each conversation.

You can only apply pressure when there is a solid structure (re-read Chapter 5 on the 'Daily structure'). Negotiators are expected to achieve a MINIMUM of 40 viewings a week, so micromanage the viewing figures in both the morning and afternoon ring-round sessions; if the negotiators do not achieve this level of viewings then your business will fail! Not only will it produce fewer sales, but the whole process of maintaining a level of service to your vendors will also fail. You will be back watching those all-important DNA tests before you know it!

More viewings means more feedback and so better constructive advice for the vendors. A good manager should lead by example and be available to cover viewing tours for the negotiators during prime times. Plus it helps to get personal feedback from the applicants.

As I have previously stated, it's not how long a property has been on the market but how many people have seen it that realises its true value. How can you advise vendors that their property is on the market for too much money and recommend a price reduction if only two people have seen it? On the other hand, if 20 people have seen it and you are armed with the feedback from every viewing, you are now in a position to advise the vendors correctly, from simply tidying up to a price reduction.

It's important that your negotiators stick to the daily structure, so you should help with sales progression. As a rule, the office manager will generally get better results and responses when dealing with people in the legal profession.

Setting realistic targets for each individual is the best way to micromanage your office. So many managers and companies set simple targets, such as two sales per week per negotiator, without helping each negotiator to achieve this. As more viewings equals more offers, and in turn more sales, set realistic targets and help the negotiators to achieve them.

If in the current climate it takes ten viewings (people not properties) to create an offer (stats are very important so that you can adapt the basic formula accordingly), and two offers to reach one sale, then it requires 40 viewings to generate two sales! (I should have been a rocket scientist with a degree in aeronautical engineering.) Alternatively, eight (genuine) viewings a day = four offers a week = two sales a week.

Concentrate on training the negotiators to achieve the level of viewings it requires to meet their sales targets, checking after the morning and afternoon ring-rounds. This is micromanaging. Do not let your negotiators get caught up in emailing or updating the system (aargh!). Get them to PICK THE PHONE UP!

If my negotiators were not on the phone during prime time, I would strap the phone to the side of their head with an elastic band! (Isn't that right, Dunner Fish?)

Sell the viewing and the property will sell itself!

VALUATIONS

The more properties you have to sell, the more applicants you will attract to sell to. As your property database grows so will your applicant level.

It used to be easy for the agents with the most properties to find themselves at the top of the list on property portals (Rightmove, Zoopla, etc.), but with these sites' haste to be buyer-friendly rather than estate-agent-friendly, it really is back to the good old 'AA Plumbers' syndrome (or listing in alphabetical order), so if you are thinking of opening your own estate agency one day I suggest you call it AAAAAARGH! Estates.

Valuing a house is based entirely on what other similar properties have sold for recently within the area. The London market has become Americanised in its approach, basing sales valuations on price per square foot (or metre if you're modern!). Outside of London the housing market currently still relies on the estate agent's opinion, but I'm pretty sure it will soon follow suit.

In London, estate agents value houses using a simple calculation of pounds per square foot minus the cost of any works needed. For example, a house in Notting Hill in West London may cost you £1,500 per square foot in good condition. If the property is 1,000 square feet then the value is £1.5m.

If, however, the property needs modernising and the work has been calculated at a rate of £150 per square foot then you would reduce the asking price by £150,000. Simples!

So, if all the agents are armed with the same 'simples!' information, how do vendors choose who to instruct?

If the potential vendors have had contact with your office prior to the valuation, the service that your staff provided should make instructing you a formality. If it's not, time to ask why not and learn from it. Perhaps a case of, "A man who knows nothing and knows not that he knows nothing is a fool. A man who knows nothing and knows that he knows nothing, teach him and he will be wise." See, I learnt something from that Buddhist Monk in Chiswick all those years ago.

However, if this is the first contact – I shouldn't need to write this but I will – think PRESENTATION and APPEARANCE! As a non-smoker the first thing I notice when meeting someone who does smoke is the smell. I can even walk past someone in a supermarket and can tell that they smoke. I am definitely not one of those ex-smokers who thinks their shit don't stink, but the smell is repulsive to those who don't smoke (the smoke not the shit). I have seen valuers and managers on their way to do valuations have a quick sneaky fag beforehand! DON'T!

Basically, smarten your presentation and appearance. A suit and for men a tie is a must, polished shoes, combed hair, etc. The first estate agency I worked for made us wear our jackets at all times, even in the hottest of summers. (Thank goodness for all those air conditioning units, NOT!) Ironically, we were allowed to smoke at our desks!

Just like registering applicants, the most important information you need from your vendors is MOTIVATION. Why are they moving? Before you walk round the property and start talking about values, discuss their circumstances. Without knowing your vendors, how can you match them to the perfect buyer?

Vendors come with many different reasons and priorities: downsizing, upsizing, moving abroad, changing schools, in a rush, no rush, and so on. You must understand these reasons before you go any further. (Don't forget to stroke the dog and write down the children's names.)

The valuation visit

Once you have established the reasons for moving, and you have sympathetically discussed the options, you may proceed to look around the property, but only pointing out the positives! Ask questions that may help with potential buyers, such as:

"Have you ever considered building a conservatory on the back?", "Have you considered converting the loft?" or "When was the boiler last serviced?"

Knowing the answers to such questions about the property you are showing to a potential buyer always sounds a lot better than "I dunno!" or making up some terrible story that only your mother would believe. (Never forget that potential buyers equal future vendors.)

Go armed with KNOWLEDGE. Always provide evidence of comparable properties that have sold recently in the area during your sales pitch. Make it personal and explain who the people were and why they sold their property through you for such an exceptional price. Comparing similar situations helps to build a rapport with potential vendors.

Most people will instruct the estate agent that they feel they can have a working relationship with and who can prove they are knowledgeable and successful. Always try to find common ground (as detailed in Chapter 3 'Getting to know your applicants'.) I cannot stress how important this is.

During a valuation always discuss with the vendors any potential buyers that you have registered in the office. Mention them by name and outline their circumstances, matching them to the vendors' situation and explaining why they would be perfect for their property. The more personally you build the relationship, the better chance you have of being instructed to sell their home. (Note, stroke the dog again.)

Discuss the office daily structure and how this will benefit the vendors. Remember, the more people who see the property in a short period of time, the better the chances of achieving the maximum price or determining whether the property has been marketed at the correct price, based on applicant feedback.

The biggest issue that the majority of vendors have with estate agents is the lack of feedback. Agree with the vendors at the time of the valuation whether they would prefer feedback after every viewing or weekly.

Always provide constructive feedback, NOT along the lines of, "The applicant liked it but wants a three-bedroom house and your house only has two bedrooms." You're likely to be faced with a vehement response: "Then why the fuck show them my house in the first place!?" Think before you speak!

Constructive feedback includes, for example, that the applicant likes the property but has seen slightly bigger houses for the same money, or that the property needs too much work for the price. This is not negative but simply reality and it's feedback that the vendors can do something about, such as dropping the price or redecorating. Telling the vendors that the second bedroom is too small ain't very helpful, me ole china!

The price and the fee
The subject agents fear the most is… the fee! Fees vary dramatically across the country and agents structure the way

fees are paid differently. In London, any decent agent will charge between 2 and 2.5 per cent. But don't be complacent. If you can't negotiate the fee with the vendors then how can you possibly negotiate the best price for them? (It helps here to stroke the dog again.)

There are some agents who have never negotiated their fees and happen to be the most successful agents in London. Realistically, the lower the fees, the lower the commission and the lower the calibre of the negotiators. But that's just my opinion!

Fight for your fee. Everything I have told you about providing the best service, calling people back, arranging a high level of viewings, giving people the correct advice, prime time ring-rounds and the rest will eventually lead to good recommendations; and when you are highly recommended by other clients or buyers then the art of negotiation gets a lot easier. Trust me…

Once you start down the slippery road of reducing your fee, the quality of the property you are instructed to sell will also slip. Wouldn't you prefer to have a reputation for being *the best at what you do*? Well, for that you have to charge the best.

Take a look at Foxtons (the brand), perhaps a swear word within the industry but they are without a doubt the most successfully marketed estate agency, from signwritten Mini Coopers driving around every chic London street, to glass-fronted monuments-to-god-sized offices. "Is that a trendy coffee shop? No, it's Foxtons!" Let's face it, John Hunt sold the company for £370,000,000 (yes, that's three hundred and seventy million pounds)… and they never reduced their fees under his reign.

My recommendation is never to put a value on the property at the first valuation meeting. Spend the time building your relationship, as above; plus it's always good to have a second bite at the cherry. Some vendors could possibly, even after experiencing your charming personality, decide not to instruct you there and then solely based on your valuation and fee structure. I always preferred to be the last valuation they received so I could discuss what the other valuations were and what fees the other agents were proposing. Naughty, but effective!

When you do call the potential vendors to discuss the price, justify the reasons why you have valued their property at that price. With all the technology available today and portal systems it's a lot easier, plus most vendors have the same access to such information as you and the majority will have already done their homework.

In my own company we would not tie our vendors into a contract for any length of time. We took the attitude that if they were not happy with the service we provided, they could terminate the contract immediately.

Outside of the London area most agents will charge the vendors upfront costs for photography and floor plans, as much as £1,000, and will try to lock the vendors into a long-term contract. What would you prefer to offer during your newly inspired drive to *be the best at what you do*?

Promoting the property

Securing interested applicants via the internet grows year on year so presenting the property online in its best light is very important. As the manager you must act as a quality controller. Every day for an hour look through the property portals and make sure your instructions stand out. If not, change the photos, make changes to the descriptions and compare the asking prices. Remember the photo is the first thing applicants will see of the property – does the photo inspire you to look further at the details? Ask yourself if the properties you have advertised look too expensive. Especially with the lettings market, applicants will tend to call about the cheaper properties first.

Regularly check other agents' websites to compare what they are advertising. There may possibly be a property you recognise.

If the property is outside the London boroughs of Westminster and Kensington & Chelsea (where the councils do not allow boards) the presence of a board is extremely important. Many vendors will ask for a board not to be erected, but in my opinion a good percentage of properties are sold because of the presence of a board. It also, of course, helps to build the brand (name awareness) and gain further instructions.

There is no better advert than a 'For Sale' board being erected and then changing a few weeks later to an 'Under Offer' board. Brand awareness is key and the agent with the greater board presence will be perceived as the greater agent.

Hark back to when I said people are like sheep and the 'if it's good enough for them then it's good enough for me' syndrome.

Added value

If the vendors are looking to move within the area then during the sale valuation arrange for them to view some suitable properties with you or with one of the negotiators who you feel would be best suited to deal with them. You are continuing to build a rapport and helping them to move throughout the whole process. You might be surprised to learn that most agents do not provide this service, perhaps due to a lack of training and knowledge. Thank goodness for your *Trust Me…* manual!

If after these simple steps you are still failing to gain instructions, don't worry, there is always recruitment!

PS

When returning to the office with a new instruction to give to the sales team for the ring-round, try to avoid the phrase, "I just got a semi on!"

– 12 –

ADVERTISING AND MARKETING

Generally, the advertising and marketing within an estate agency is dealt with by a separate department, but you will be responsible for the content, the photo quality and the descriptions, for example.

In most cases this information will be taken from the already prepared details (property description). Before property portals such as Onthemarket, Rightmove and Zoopla, we only had our window display and the 'squeaking rages' (Yellow Pages) to attract potential customers.

Now that the whole world can view your available properties and the company's presentation (the brand), you must check and double-check that all the information you are providing is correct and that the property is being shown in the best possible light.

Would you instruct agents to sell your house if they couldn't spell a local road correctly?

The types of property you will be selling in the future are the types of properties you are marketing today!

Quite simply, the more properties you advertise, the more applicants you will attract within a certain price range. It is common for different agents to be better at selling properties in certain price ranges. You wouldn't sell a small studio flat through Savills, for example!

Look at the market that you feel is best suited for your agency and base your advertising on promoting this.

Features such as a 'Just sold on your street' are good marketing tools. Everyone likes to know what's happening in their area, and let's face it we are all nosey neighbours. Write to all the addresses on the street informing them of your latest or potential sale, or your 'just exchanged on your street', 'just agreed on your street', etc.

You will find that local people have friends moving to the area, so why not send out 'just been instructed on your street' flyers? If nothing else it will increase your brand awareness.

Negotiators must be up to date with all the local applicants who are PTS (see Chapter 1) as this is the best source of instructions. PTS applicants must be called weekly. You may, as a manager, want to look after potential vendors yourself. If you make a diary note of the time every week in your schedule to call, then call back exactly when you say you will, this shows good organisation.

Depending on the housing climate, you will want to attract either more vendors or more buyers. If there is a property shortage then focus your advertising on properties that you have recently sold (ideally the ones you have achieved an exceptional price for). If, however, there is an abundance of property on the market for sale then focus your advertising on available property.

The housing market is seasonal, so it would not be the best advice for vendors to start marketing their property at the end of November, too close to Christmas. Many buyers change their focus at that time to shops and shopping centres, and who wants to move at Christmas? Direct your advertising campaign for new instructions to be marketed from January: new year, new leaf, time to move.

I don't believe that many sales are achieved through magazine and newspaper advertising, although they are great to promote the brand of the company, your profile and the types of property that you deal with on a daily basis. Try not to offer what I call 'bucket advertising', or the same package as every other agent, with pages and pages of half-decent photos and boring, repetitive descriptions.

Potential vendors will look through the local property papers, magazines and websites to help them choose which agents they want to come and value their property.

Our best advertising campaign, 'The Time to Move', was images of all the reasons why people move, from a positive pregnancy test to a sink full of dirty dishes! Try to think of adverts outside of that bucket!

Social media is a complex business, especially for those of my generation and beyond. Think Facebook, Twitter, LinkedIn, Instagram, not to mention your own website.

Similar to the 'bucket' of magazine advertising, what makes your social media content stand out from your competitors? The most followed Twitter account belongs to Rihanna (an American singer, actress and fashion designer) and I am sure the majority of followers aren't looking at her next tour dates! In that case, photos of pot-smoking, naked ring-rounds will definitely make you stand out from the rest. They might not achieve the desired results though.

The best way to describe the power of social media is that you are now promoting the 'brand' and not just individual properties. Interesting photos, funny situations, promotions, giveaways and local sponsorships and events all have a part to play. Estate agency is considered a boring subject in the world of social media, so a good campaign or ongoing scenario will help to increase your followers, perhaps 'The worst photos of the week' or 'Vendors' pets', for example.

Let's face it, most of us are salespeople so we employ social media companies to post the pictures and tweet the tweets etc. across all the appropriate media sites; but just remember that you are more than likely the person responsible for the content.

THE 'LESLIE CROWTHER'

Why is our industry full of jargon, you ask? Here's a tale from my past.

On a lazy summer's Friday afternoon the manager (the one who liked to call me "son") and the sales negotiators would call all the vendors to discuss potentially reducing the asking price of their properties (generally because the manager had overpriced the properties in the first place just to gain the instructions – not a practice I recommend today!).

This was 1984, when a television show was launched in the UK called *The Price is Right*, hosted by no other than Mr Leslie Crowther, a TV presenter that Mr Chan of Emlyn Road in Chiswick had not heard of until now.

From my front desk I could hear one side of a telephone conversation going on behind me:

"Mr Chan, unfortunately the price isn't right, you're gonna have to give me a Leslie Crowther."

Then came a long pause.

I believe a very confused and surprised Mr Chan responded: "Wat is a Weswie Cwowther?"

Now, the famous presenter had a famous saying when you were picked from the audience to play in the game show: "Mr... Come on down!" So it was to follow.

"Mr Chan, the price isn't right, you've gotta come on down!"

Needless to say, Mr Chan no longer required our professional services to sell his house. Funnily enough, we no longer had the Price Reduction Afternoon either. Instead the Leslie Crowther Afternoon was born.

And I believe it's still used in some remote parts of London today...

– FINAL PS –

Be careful out there!

– INDEX –

Printed in Great Britain
by Amazon

23694166R00066